LIVI

HEIDI BAKER
WITH SHARA PRADHAN

Edited by Frank A. DeCenso Jr.

DESTINY IMAGE PUBLISHERS

Scripture is the authors' own. Please note that Destiny Image's publishing style capitalizes certain pronouns in Scripture that refer to the Father, Son, and Holy Spirit, and may differ from some publishers' styles. Take note that the name satan and related names are not capitalized. We choose not to acknowledge him, even to the point of violating grammatical rules.

DESTINY IMAGE® PUBLISHERS, INC.

P.O. Box 310, Shippensburg, PA 17257-0310

"Speaking to the Purposes of God for this Generation and for the Generations to Come."

This book and all other Destiny Image, Revival Press, Mercy Place, Fresh Bread, Destiny Image Fiction, and Treasure House books are available at Christian bookstores and distributors worldwide.

For a U.S. bookstore nearest you, call 1-800-722-6774.

For more information on international availability, call 717-532-3040.

Reach us on the Internet at www.destinyimage.com.

Physical Edition ISBN: 978-0-7684-1627-5

Digital Edition ISBN: 978-0-7684-1613-8

Originally published in *God's Supernatural Power in You* ISBN 978-0-7684-2832-2.

Living Under Water

Heidi Baker
with Shara Pradhan

THE SECRET TO REVIVAL

Therefore, my brethren, you also have become dead to the law through the body of the Christ, that you may be married to another—to Him who was raised from the dead, that we should bear fruit to God (Romans 7:4).

People often ask, "What is the secret to revival?" The secret place is the secret to revival. In the midst of my busy life overseeing thousands of churches, caring for thousands of children, and feeding thousands of people every day, Jesus spoke to me to reverse my schedule. He wants our time. He said, "I want you to come away, my beloved. I want to woo you. I want to love you. I want you to live in this secret place. If you give me your mornings, I will give you a nation."

Holy Passion

My commissioning to the nations started by being called as His Bride. Many years ago, Jesus came to me in a vision. A bright white light surrounded me, and I heard the external, audible voice of God for the first time in my life. I was 16 years old. Jesus said that I was to be married to Him. Oil ran down my arm, and I felt Him kiss my left ring finger. He said, "You are called to be a minister and a missionary. You are called to Africa, Asia, and England." When the presence of God lifted, I was alone in the church. I had been still with my hands raised for nearly three hours. Incredible joy hit me, and I began to preach the next day. I have been preaching and living a life of missions ever since. God called me to give my life for the poor.

My husband, Rolland, and I have been missionaries for 28 years in Asia, Europe, and Africa. Since that divine commissioning, I have preached the Gospel. And still the Lord speaks to me to simplify. Still the Lord says that He wants more of my time. He asks me for my mornings. I live in the holy chaos of overseeing Iris Ministries and caring for so many children in our beloved Village of Joy in Pemba, Mozambique. And at times, I hear God saying, "Come away, my beloved and walk on the beach; come and ride your bike with me; come and lay down in my presence." And my little religious heart is thumping as I get overwhelmed by the ever-present needs.

One of my life passages is John 15, which is about abiding in Jesus, remaining in the vine so that our lives can bear much fruit. I know that God, as the master vine dresser, wants to prune and chop away things that are religious to draw us into the secret place of His heart. Revival is impossible outside of divine union and communion with Him. He is not as concerned with how much we can do for Him as with how much holy passion fills our hearts for Him. Lovers outwork workers. There is nothing I would not gladly give my King. And God responds, "In that case, I want your time."

Living Under Water

And it shall be that every living thing that moves, wherever the rivers go, will live. There will be a very great multitude of fish, because these waters go there; for they will be healed, and everything will live wherever the river goes. It shall be that fishermen will stand by it from En Gedi to En Eglaim; they will be places for spreading their nets. Their fish will be of the

> *same kinds as the fish of the Great Sea, exceedingly many. But its swamps and marshes will not be healed; they will be given over to salt. Along the bank of the river, on this side and that, will grow all kinds of trees used for food; their leaves will not wither, and their fruit will not fail. They will bear fruit every month, because their water flows from the sanctuary. Their fruit will be for food, and their leaves for medicine* (Ezekiel 47:9-12).

I live to spend time with Him. I live to be fully possessed by His glorious presence. God yearns to draw us so deeply into this Ezekiel 47 river that we do bear fruit all 12 months of the year, that our lives do bring healing to the nations, that we go beyond ankle, knee, or waist deep; we go until we are fully immersed in the ocean of His liquid love. Only from this place of full possession can we truly be used by Him.

I take this passage in the book of Ezekiel quite literally! When God told me that He wanted more of my time, I rearranged my daily schedule in Mozambique so that I do not start before 11 in the morning, except for times of prayer. I love to wake up really early to the African sunrise and spend hours with my Jesus. The more people press in with needs and crises, the more I must press into His presence. The greater the daily challenges, the more I must pray. Every day, I must seek His face and worship Him.

Sometimes I stick on a snorkel and swim out in the turquoise, tropical, clear Indian Ocean. I swim out away from the never-ending cues, lists of demands, and ever-present crises. Deep, deep in the water, I am finally alone with Him. I love swimming into that silent underwater garden where I am away from everyone else, and I can hear His still small whisper. I worship under water and admire His beautiful creation. I delight in being alone with Him—just Jesus, me, and often a bright yellow little fish. An hour may pass by as I simply pray, "Lord Jesus Christ, beautiful Son of God, have mercy on me, your beloved." Some might look upon this and think that I am being lazy. Some might even think I am irresponsible to go snorkeling or riding my bike when there are still hungry people to be fed, churches to oversee, and children to care for. But the more I have to do, the more I must press into prayer. I have no choice but to be utterly dependent on Him.

I have to live in the secret place of His heart. In Pemba, every week we see villages run to Jesus. Since the Lord spoke to me five years ago to move to Cabo Delgado, in order to get His lost Makua bride, we are seeing village after village love Him. The Makua tribe was the most unreached people group in southeast Africa, according to missiologists. Since Jesus sent our ragtag Iris family of missionaries and Mozambicans to Pemba, we have seen hundreds and hundreds of churches planted among this tribe. Most weeks, Jesus opens up deaf ears as He is opening the ears of our nation to hear the good news of the Gospel of Jesus Christ. Each day, He miraculously provides food for the hungry. Each day, I watch His Kingdom break forth with His glorious light in spite of challenges too great to tell. Weekly, we have crises and problems which would make your heart faint. But He brings peace in the storms. And in the midst of it, we see Jesus.

Yet even as we see revival break forth, Jesus told me that His favorite time of my day is the mornings. He loves it when I snorkel or ride my bike or simply lay down in a quiet place with my heart fixed on Him. I love to pray in that underwater garden. I love to pray while looking at His beauty. It is just me adoring Him. I do not pray through a list of intercessory needs, though that is a good thing to do. I do not tell Him how to feed the people, because He knows how to feed them.

I want to know nothing but Christ and Christ crucified (see 1 Cor. 2:2). I just swim or ride or rest and love Him: "Holy, holy, holy. Worthy, worthy, worthy. I love you! I love you!" And He spoke to me, "Heidi, this morning time is my favorite time of our day." He loves our intimacy more than miracles, more than seeing villages saved, and even more than seeing orphans fed. Like Romans 7:4 teaches, in order for us to bear fruit to God, we must be intimate with Jesus. All fruitfulness flows from that place of laid-down love. All fruitfulness flows from intimacy.

God longs to be loved. He wants to know that He is more important than revival. He must be more of a priority than the multitudes, than the fruit, than the miracles. When we are that in love with Him, fruit happens. It is effortless in love.

I have one goal and that is to be such an intimate lover of Jesus that I am a resting place for the Holy Spirit. I want to be so one with Him that I become like Him, love like Him, and radiate His very nature until I become a resting place for His presence. More happens in one single minute in the anointing than in a lifetime of labor and efforts. We can do nothing by our own efforts. It is not by might, not by power, but only by His spirit (see Zech. 4:6).

We can do nothing apart from His presence. Like my morning snorkel swim or bike ride, our entire ministry must flow from His Holy Spirit. There is a place in the Spirit where you can cast out the Ezekiel 47 nets when you live inside the very heart of Jesus. Only then can you spread out nets so that Jesus can catch fish from every tribe and tongue. Only then can we be like those fruit trees which bring fruit all year long. Only then can our lives truly bring healing to the nations.

The water in this passage flows from the sanctuary. Likewise, our whole lives must flow from the holy of holies. God does not want a worship service but unceasing union and communion. We must give never-ending adoration to our King Jesus. When we live from this place of being fully submerged in the ocean of His liquid love, we will bear fruit to bring healing to the nations. There is a place of supernatural fruitfulness where our lives are so deep in His glory that exponential fruit pops out of each one of our little laid down lives of love.

If you are not in love, you should quit.

First Commandment First

The first step in ministry is to be intimate with Jesus. Our greatest joy in life is to be married to Jesus so that we can give our lives away without fear, just as He did for us. My goal, even in this chapter, is that you would fall so deeply in love that there would be no "no" left in you when responding to the high calling of God. When you are so full of the presence of God, when a person meets you, they meet Him. When you hold them, Jesus holds them. Then Jesus becomes irresistible to them.

Missions, ministry, and revival are defined by laid-down passion at the foot of the cross. There we pray, "Possess me, Holy Spirit, that I might be conformed into Your image. Let me reflect the majesty of who You are."

Love God and Your Neighbor

My mission statement for Iris Ministries for nearly three decades is simple: love God, love our neighbor. This is the five-year plan. This is the 10-year plan. This is the 20-year everything message.

Love God with all your heart, mind, soul, and spirit, and love your neighbor as yourself (see Luke 10:27). Be one with each other and one with

Christ Jesus. To make this possible, Jesus died and rose from the dead.

What is God's goal? He wants every single person in this world to know Him. He wants every man, woman, and child to be taken in as His sons and daughters. He wants His house to be full.

He made Heaven big enough for everyone. Because He died, there is always enough. How can the Gospel go forth to the ends of the earth so that none should perish? Paul the apostle answered this very question by writing, *"fulfill my joy by being like-minded, having the same love, being of one accord, of one mind"* (Phil. 2:2). This is the reason why we give up our homes, our families, our possessions. It is not so that we will look like we are doing something good. We give everything to God as we follow the Lamb who was slain. He gave everything to us. We choose our lover. We choose to be married to Him. If we choose Him, then in Him, we have all that we need.

A New Breed of Ministers

Missions is not about where you are; it is about where He is.

Love knows no limits, places, or bounds.

Revival starts with seeking His face.

A new breed of ministers is rising up; they will not wear out for the Gospel. They are so caught up in passion, union, unity, and fullness that they will run out and say, "Congo, here I come!" And if they get shot at, they are thrilled. And if they don't get shot at, they are thrilled. If the place is filthy, they are thrilled. If it is clean, they are thrilled (see Phil. 4:11-12). He is the joy set before them (see Heb. 12:2). He is their exceedingly great reward. Their lives are full of joy unspeakable and full of glory (see 1 Pet. 1:8).

The secret of revival is the secret place. Missions is not about where you go; it is about where He is. He has to move on the inside of you. You have to feel His heart before you will have anything to offer anyone else. Then, when you have rested your very head against His chest, like John the beloved, you can move according to His heartbeat.

Despite traveling hundreds of thousands of kilometers last year, I find myself at home wherever I am. And I find myself at home everywhere I go. When I am in Korea, I love Korea! When I am in Brazil, I am Brazilian! Of course, Mozambique is my favorite place on earth. It is truly home. When I know that God sent me somewhere, I am happy there. I live for Him. It is all about this passion; it is all about where He is. The most important things for me are union with Him and embracing the one in front of me.

Joy in the Holy Spirit

For the kingdom of God is not eating and drinking, but righteousness and peace and joy in the Holy Spirit (Romans 14:17).

Ministers should be the most joyful, in-love people on the planet. The Gospel is not a competition in misery. I remember living in Asia where missionaries seemed to compete to see who could be the most miserable. Many would boast in their newsletters about how difficult it was suffering for the Gospel. From their perspective, the one who suffered the most would surely get brownie points in Heaven for misery. I have been shot at five times, I have been beaten and thrown in jail, and I have fasted often. I know a bit about suffering and pain. And yet, I count it as nothing. I count it as joy (see James 1:2). If you want to export misery, then find another profession. Joy is contagious. If we are not full of Him, we have nothing to offer anyone else.

Unstoppable in Love

Ministry ought to be the most contagious, outrageous, Holy Spirit adventure this side of Heaven.

In October 2005, I almost died in the hospital from a MRSA infection. I determined that I would not die in that way! I would not die of a dirty, flesh-eating disease. I want to be a martyr for Jesus one day.

However, it is easy to die for Jesus, and it is more difficult to live fully for Him. I do not want to just die well; I want to live well. Until my last breath, I want to give everything that I am for all that He is. As Mother Teresa wrote, "You love until there is pain; you love through the pain until all that remains is love."

If you are really in love, then it is a joy to suffer for the Gospel. If you feel pain, get deeper and closer to His heart. Press in for the face-to-face presence. Nothing will seem difficult when He is only a breath away.

The amount of crises that we deal with at Iris in any one day is ridiculous. If we were not in love, we would be in a mental institute! But we are not in a mental institute because we are in love.

When crises come to me and press in on me, one after another, I just have to look into the eyes of the One I love. He is always enough!

I want to be fully possessed by His Holy Spirit until I am completely overshadowed by God. I want to be utterly overtaken. My prayer is that we would all stay hidden inside of God's glorious heart of love until we are manifesting His nature as sons and daughters, living, breathing, moving, healing, and giving life to others just as Jesus did. My prayer is that we would not even pursue power, but His presence, that we would not only seek revival, but also His face, that we would determine to live in the secret place of His heart.

The Fire of His Eyes

Set me as a seal upon your heart, as a seal upon your arm; for love is as strong as death, jealousy as cruel as the grave; its flames are flames of fire, a most vehement flame. Many waters cannot quench love, nor can the floods drown it... (Song of Solomon 8:6-7).

Many do not know how to live in the secret place. Many do not understand intimacy. Beloved, it is simpler than we think. It is just about letting Him love us.

Every time I have had a vision or impression of Jesus, I have always been undone by His eyes of love. They are like liquid flames of fiery love. Many waters cannot quench this love. Focus on His face, Church. Focus on His heart, Bride. If we have the courage to lock gazes with Him, He can purify our hearts. When He looks into us with His eyes like a flame of fire, eternity is branded on our hearts.

We must behold His face to become like Him. Then we can dwell in the fire of His embrace. Isaiah 33:14-15 reads, *"...Who among us shall dwell with the devouring fire? Who among us shall dwell with everlasting burnings? He who walks righteously....*" To dwell in this fire, we must fix our eyes on Jesus. Then, when people peer into our eyes, Jesus will look back at them.

I believe God wants to pour out fresh salve to give us His eyes to see and His ears to hear a lost and dying world. We have made our God too small; we imagine that He has limits. When we do not have His eyes, we start to see God in our image rather than seeing humanity in the image of God. We must have pure eyes to see God for who He is. When we see God for who He truly is, we will want to be pure. And we will know that He is big enough for all of our needs. You cannot meet all of your needs because you are not God. God is God, and we are not!

When we see with God's perspective, it is so much bigger than our own. Recently I had another visitation. I was picked up by two angels, one on each side, and we began to fly across the nations of the earth. The angels handed me golden oil as I saw multitudes of sick, dying, and broken people. I flew with the angels over nations and poured this liquid, golden oil like honey upon the people. They all fell on their faces. Everyone was healed. I saw this huge, incredible harvest like nothing I had ever seen before. I am now beginning to experience this harvest and the fulfillment of that vision. His heart is big enough to love the entire world.

Again, the secret to revival is the secret place. The secret to fruitfulness is intimacy. We must remain in God if God is to remain in us. It is impossible to bear fruit outside of life in the vine. In a time when He is shaking everything that can be shaken (see Hag. 2:6-7) and ministers and ministries are being tested and pruned, we must finish well in Him.

God wants more time with us. The only way to run the race well is to look at Jesus. When we fix our gaze only on Him, all things are possible. God is looking today not only for powerful people, but for intimate lovers who are so overshadowed with His presence that His glory may hover over them.

The more time we spend with God, the more fruitfulness will happen in our lives. Our ministries will be greater than what we have ever dreamed of. We must not look at our inability but gaze into the eyes of the Only Able One. We are never able on our own. It is all about Him. He is able. So let Him draw you past the outer courts into the Holy of Holies. Go so deep, past the knees, past the waist, until you are in over your head.

Final Prayer: Abide in Him

Let Him love you. It is so much simpler than we thought. It is time to be transformed by His love so that there is no fear in you. Be wrecked for everything but His presence. Be so utterly and abandoned in His love.

God in His glory will pour His presence into people to the degree that entire nations will be transformed. He will pour His love out like a river, like an ocean. Let Him kiss you with the kisses of His mouth. Dive into His heart.

It's time to lie down and let God be God. He is mighty, and nothing is impossible with Him. He wants to kiss His church, and transform you with His love. We are called to be carriers of His glory. It is not about being an eloquent speaker, man of power for the hour, or great revivalist. It is about being so close to the heart of God that you know what He's thinking. Then you are not afraid to go anywhere and say anything as His radical lovers. He captivates us so that we can never go back. He wants to shatter your box.

Often our God is still too small. It is time for whole nations.

Lie down so that He can trust you with everyone. Then when you get up there is revival—when whole nations come to Him, falling on their faces. He changes us with one glance of His eyes, so that we are not afraid to be completely abandoned in His arms. Many want lots of power and anointing, but when we just lie down and let Him love us to death and kiss us back to life, it is a truly powerful thing.

He is looking for union, not occasional worship so that our very nature is transformed. We must walk in His nature, and we must die daily.

Again all fruitfulness flows from intimacy. To the degree that we are untied with the heart of Jesus, God will bring fruit in our lives. To the degree that we are in love with Him, we will be fruitful. We cannot make revival happen. But we can become so hungry for God, we become a prisoner of love. And these prisoners of love, these harvesters, will so carry His glorious presence, the hungry can no longer resist anymore.

> *I am the true vine, and My Father is the vinedresser. Every branch in Me that does not bear fruit He*

takes away; and every branch that bears fruit He prunes, that it may bear more fruit. You are already clean because of the word which I have spoken to you. Abide in Me, and I in you. As the branch cannot bear fruit of itself, unless it abides in the vine, neither can you, unless you abide in Me. I am the vine, you are the branches. He who abides in Me, and I in him, bears much fruit; for without Me you can do nothing. If anyone does not abide in Me, he is cast out as a branch and is withered; and they gather them and throw them into the fire, and they are burned. If you abide in Me, and My words abide in you, you will ask what you desire, and it shall be done for you. By this My Father is glorified, that you bear much fruit; so you will be My disciples. As the Father loved Me, I also have loved you; abide in My love. If you keep My commandments, you will abide in My love, just as I have kept My Father's commandments and abide in His love. These things I have spoken to you, that My joy may remain in you, and that your joy may be full. This is My commandment, that you love one another as I have loved you. Greater love has no one than this, than to lay down one's life for his friends. You are My friends if you do whatever I command you. No longer do I call you servants, for a servant does not know what his master is doing; but I have called you friends, for all things that I heard from My Father I have made known to you. You did not choose Me, but I chose you and appointed you that you should go and bear fruit, and that your fruit should remain, that whatever you ask the Father in My name He may give you (John 15:1-16).

About Heidi Baker

Dr. Heidi Baker and her husband, Rolland, are the founders and directors of Iris Ministries. God has given them a heart for the poor, and they have been missionaries for the last 23 years in Asia, Europe, and Africa. For the past eight years, they have been ministering in the nation of Mozambique, where they are caring for orphans and street children while seeing a glorious revival in which thousands of churches have been planted.

Although Heidi holds a BA and MA from S.C.C., Vanguard University and a PhD in Systematic Theology from King's College, University of London, she learned more on the floor, under the weighty glory of Jesus for seven days and seven nights in Toronto, than in 10 years of university. Jesus told her, "You can do nothing without Me and nothing without the Body of Christ."

One third of Heidi's time is spent travelling throughout the nations preaching on passion for Jesus. Her heart is to impart His huge heart of love. Heidi loves Jesus more than life. Her life message is that all fruitfulness flows out of intimacy with Him (see John 14 and 15).

Notes

Printed in Great Britain
by Amazon

71261008R00037